THE FUTURE NEVER SPEAKS

THE SEARCH FOR MEANING IN HISTORY

By Richard Grassby

2nd edition revised

Priestess Pythia, keeper of Apollo's oracle at Delphi

"The Future—never spoke—

Nor will He—like the Dumb—

Reveal by sign—a syllable

Of His Profound To Come"

(Emily Dickinson)

TABLE OF CONTENTS

Preface

Introduction: The Questions of History.

I. What is known to have taken place?

II. Where and when did it occur?

III. Who brought it about?

IV. What were the driving forces?

V. Whether it should be preserved or condemned?

VI. How did it develop?

VII. Why did it happen?.

Epilogue. Is History created by accident or by design?

Historical Works by Richard Grassby

PREFACE

Although this work stands on its own and advances new ideas and arguments, I have also drawn on material formerly included in the fourth edition of my autobiography, *A Scholar's Tale*. I thought that it was time to devote an entire book, instead of a few chapters, to my views on the writing of history.

In recent years, I have self-published many books instead of using traditional publishers, as with my earlier work. I have taken advantage of the opportunities provided by the internet and online publishers. As an independent scholar, this has been a necessity rather than a choice. Self-publication usually means that a book will not enter the mainstream in the republic of letters and consequently has a limited circulation. But it is copyrighted and is available both online, in paperback and hardback.

Why do I continue to write, when I have already published more than many historians? I persist because I enjoy finding answers to the many questions that command my attention; solving a problem is as rewarding to me as cultivating in my garden flowers which only my household or a few visitors will probably ever see.

My output may not have the exposure that conventionally published books enjoy through reviews and promotion, but my thoughts and research will be readily and permanently attainable. I like to think that my labour will be justified if just one person in the future gains some insight or is challenged or inspired by anything that I have written.

                                                      March, 2023

INTRODUCTION. THE QUESTIONS OF HISTORY

The past has long been studied because people are curious about the origins and development of the world that they inhabit. Historians, both amateur and professional, are driven by the same motives that prompt scientists to probe the origin of the universe, of the Earth, or of the human species. Many historians just assume that their research is important and valid and focus on accumulating evidence and trying to make sense of it. But their objectives and methods still need justification and have become the subject of a substantial specialist literature.

Even though many similarities can be detected between past and present, the past is still a foreign country. We all inhabit the past because the present is just a marker between past and future. The moment that anything occurs, it automatically becomes the past. The past, unlike the future, can be known, but our perception of it often differs from what actually happened. Historians usually prioritize their personal agendas and see only what they want to find, whether their goal is to applaud or to condemn. History is not a report of events, but a constructed story. Historians have to recognize the facts, but they compile their own narrative. Their personality and beliefs are therefore as important as, or even more important than, the evidence.

Once humans had acquired the ability to store and transmit knowledge and ideas without relying, like animals, on inheritance, it became possible for them to look back in time. They could reconstruct the past because they could recognize and understand what their predecessors had experienced. But the future was always a mystery. Thinkers had some notion of where humanity had originated and how it had evolved, but no clear idea of where it might be heading.

Anyone serious about studying History must challenge all assumptions, question everything and take nothing for granted. The facts do have to be unearthed and marshaled, and they are best derived from first hand material rather than from secondary sources. Ideally historians, like journalists, distinguish between description and analysis; they report the news on the main pages and connect the dots and comment on them in editorials or opinion pieces. So we can state with complete confidence that Napoleon died at Saint Helena, but we do not know for certain why he lost the battle of Waterloo.

But readers expect results. A reviewer of one of Gerald Aylmer's dense volumes on Stuart bureaucracy once complained that he could not find a conclusion anywhere. The truth is often boring, similarity and repetition can be dull, and compromise lacks an edge. What sells is not a messy or confusing depiction of events, but clarity and certainty and movement and force.

Historians may want to seek the truth but they also want to win their case. Like advocates trying to persuade a jury in a court of law, they are tempted to shape the facts and ignore or downplay doubtful evidence. More research and increased knowledge does not, moreover, lead to greater understanding, if it is subordinated to an ideology. **All ideologies encourage extremism, disparage compromise and pervert the truth.**

The real world is analog because there are an infinite number of choices and possibilities and events,; the story of humankind relates like a stream of consciousness. The past world, as recreated and described by historians is, in contrast, digital, precise, accurate and finite. Binary categories are employed to make sense of complex events. Rather than offer multiple choices or interactions, everything is defined and explained by its opposite with no alternatives, no third parties, no middle ground. Particular facts are manipulated retrospectively to form a pattern or set out a theory or promote an ideology.

When the past is tempered and simplified in this way to remove uncertainty and doubt, one interpretation is embraced and its opposite or other is demonized. This is a grave error, because we need to see both sides of every issue. When looked at dispassionately, the evidence usually conflicts and what happened and why it happened is confused. The essence of the past is duality; there is usually right and wrong on both sides of any question. There are no simple answers. Contradiction and ambivalence are inherent. Many events occur in spite of, instead of because of, what is expected. They make perfect sense individually, when seen in a particular context, but they do not fit comfortably into a general picture.

History is both what has happened and what is thought or expected to have occurred. Sometimes the two overlap, but usually they contradict each other, because one is based on evidence and the other on faith or hope. Everyone and every period has both a real and a perceived history. The facts do not change – what and how and when – though they can be repressed, denied and falsified, and they tend to be either too few or too numerous. But their meaning and significance change constantly. Since they have to be selected and interpreted, the story that they tell will always be in flux. The past is constantly rewritten and reviewed to comply with whatever is fashionable in the present. Myths are often preferred to the truth, because they serve current needs.

Deciding what happened sometimes involves consideration of why some alternative event did not occur – the counterfactual proposition. Although we can only speculate as to what might have happened, if one or more factors had not been present, this approach is a valuable method of testing the validity of any account or explanation. Since just one of an infinite number of factors could have changed the course of history at any time, we should not be overconfident about the story that we relate.

To recast an axiom of Pierre-Marc-Gaston de Lévis, historians are best judged by their questions, rather than by their answers. Historians who ask what can be discovered about the past will write an anecdotal history or herstory of what happened. Those who ask where important events occurred will situate them in a particular context. Those who ask when they took place will anchor them in time. Those who ask who is responsible for events will clarify the role of individuals. Those who ask what happened without human participation will elucidate the function of impersonal forces. Those who ask how the world has developed will describe the methods by which that became possible. Those who ask why events unfolded as they did, rather than in some other way, can try to explain them and speculate about what they mean.

One can of course question the questions. Is it possible to discover and understand why events occurred in the shape and order that they did or were they just fortuitous? How do we interpret the facts without being biased or misled? Since we cannot live in the past, can we really understand it, or was life in past periods just too different? Is it an illusion or a conceit to think that we can experience the past from the standpoint of contemporaries? Is the story of

humankind fundamentally one damn fact after another, governed by no laws and following no model? **Does history have any pattern or direction? Or is everything accidental, unpredictable and chaotic?**

Many of us are inspired by the past and want or expect what happened to last forever. Yet we see it through the present. Life is a continuum in which the end is a beginning and no one can escape their past. Even animals draw on past experience, although they live in the present, driven by immediate wants and needs. We constantly

look back, follow tradition and romanticize the past, because it is an anchor against the uncertainty of the future. We know what happened in the past, whereas we are totally unaware of what will happen in the future.

When we plan for the future, we ascertain and grade our progress by comparing our present condition with the past. Historians spend much of their time verifying facts and assembling a narrative. They describe how the world has developed in the way that it has and try to explain why humans, both individually and collectively, have been successful in transforming their environment. But their principal objective is or should be analysis – the search for explanations and for meaning. Curiosity drives us to discover the direction and purpose of the human species.

The objective here, drawing on examples from periods of history with which the author is most familiar, is to isolate, clarify and explain which ideas and forces have pushed or pulled humanity. The emphasis is on what humans did achieve - not on what they ought to have attempted. Instead of speculating about and imagining an inexorable goal , this book assesses the significance of a past in which no one knew what to expect in the future. It explores History as a process which has no final end.

I WHAT IS KNOWN TO HAVE TAKEN PLACE?

The first task that historians face is to determine what actually happened. The earliest histories focused on process over time. Annals, like the Anglo Saxon Chronicle, established and recorded a narrative of the past without much documentation or commentary - what, when and where particular situations occurred. Recreating the course of events in chronological order still provides a framework to understand how the present has evolved from the past.

A simple narrative, as in the history of most institutions, shows how one event leads to another and is self explanatory. A more sophisticated approach identifies the stages that lead to major crises, such as the English Civil Wars or the French Revolution or the American Civil War, where the momentum of events is cumulative – a steady build-up until a critical mass is reached.

Facts do verify whether an event occurred, but they do not speak for themselves; they have to be selected, assembled and critically assessed. Some appear at specific moments; others have to be viewed in succession as a process or pattern. **The narrative is widened and deepened to demonstrate how events relate to each other, how they interact, merge and integrate.**

In order to understand what takes place on the surface we have to examine the underlying system at one moment of time, to show how its different sectors cohere and function. The focus might be on institutions of law and government, on the structure of a society, on a statistical model of an economy, on

a collection of habitual customs or religious beliefs, or on a value system with moral codes.

We also have to measure quantities, to compare the relative importance of factors and assess their relevance. One index of change is an increase of scale; the process may remain the same, but an increase in quantity may have qualitative significance. Although based on solid evidence and usually related to each other, these descriptive frameworks are still

projected abstractions without physical form.

The critical elements of modern historiography can be found in a few ancient authors, but the source-based narratives which currently define History trace back to intellectual and institutional developments of the late nineteenth century. Hard or soft evidence - and preferably both - is collected and examined to separate myths from reality. Stories inherited from the past are rejected when they lack any factual support or where the evidence is biased, incomplete, or ambiguous. As in a court of law, evidence may be contested, but it must ultimately be sufficient to prove a case.

The truth can only be uncovered by deep penetration of the past and preferably by unfiltered contact. The most authoritative histories are based on original, reliable and accessible sources. Every historian, however, depends on other historians for the majority of his or her facts. Most knowledge of the past is derived not from primary sources, but from information that has been processed through multiple intermediaries

and which is far removed from the original evidence.

Hard evidence is descriptive rather than analytical and it focuses on establishing the truth without pursuing irrelevant digressions. It is usually documentary, uncontested and incontrovertible and it relies on a preponderance of evidence to resolve disagreements. It establishes through multiple channels basic, concrete facts, such as a person's date and place of birth or marriage or death or education or occupation. The course of events is reconstructed by accumulating piecemeal individual details. **If hard evidence records what has been done, soft evidence repeats what people say, what they recollect having occurred. It is often indirect and circumstantial, consisting of facts revealed by third parties or inferred from situations.**

Much evidence is biased or incomplete. It may have some value, but it's worth is reduced by omissions, by a failure to see or appreciate the whole truth. Often the course of events can be established without any doubt but at other times the evidence has to be weighed and assessed. When it is one sided, it just conveys a skewed view of reality.

When the evidence conflicts, a historian may choose a version that most satisfies the expectations of his readers. National histories often suffer from this propensity, because they are expected to portray an official version of events, usually self serving and dictated by current preoccupations. Errors most commonly occur through ignorance or carelessness, but falsehoods can also be

deliberately advanced or evidence may be invented or reinvented.

The evidence is often inadequate. Most distant periods of human history and ancient civilizations have to rely on fossil records, archaeological remains and oral survivals. When written evidence is available in adequate volume and has been validated by critical appraisal, it still does not necessarily provide incontrovertible proof. Even in advanced, literate societies, many aspects of life and events are not recorded. The vast records that survive to reconstruct the past, are dwarfed by what we do not know. When the surviving evidence is insufficient or does not exist, that vacuum is filled by myths, initially transmitted orally and often organized as a religion. The earliest centuries of human history are shrouded in legend and peopled by Gods.

The accretion of knowledge is a slow process. The truth does not suddenly become manifest, but emerges cumulatively over time. It is surprisingly difficult and time consuming to verify even a relatively simple fact like the time, date and place of a person's birth or death. To understand how people

thought and felt, a historian has to immerse himself in the primary sources. The past has to be gradually reconstituted by accumulating evidence and it takes a long time to accomplish that goal, to understand and retrieve and interpret sources, to separate history from myth.

    All facts are not equal and they have to be weighed and selected in order to construct a meaningful narrative. Every historian has to have standards of importance and judge what is worth knowing and what everyone should learn.

The criteria vary between individuals and between one period and another. One incentive is natural curiosity; some topics just have intrinsic interest. Who would not want to know how the Pyramids were built, or how Hannibal took his elephants over the Alps, or how the Black Death decimated the population of the world, or how the Mongols conquered China, or how the Enigma code was broken or how Earthlings managed to walk on the moon?

    Unusual developments do fascinate and attract attention. But the majority of historians concentrate on mundane aspects of life. Some, of course, gravitate towards issues that affect them personally. A particular narrative may appeal to a historian with a taste for drama or a romantic sensibility. Past events **make most sense to those who have faced similar problems and situations in the present and who have shared similar emotions. Familiarity breeds empathy.**

What has been able to survive the passage of time and retain its value? Have we lost more than we have preserved? It is not hard to find examples of continuity. We still recognize and observe standards of morality that

emerged at the dawn of human history. Although social structures and political institutions have evolved and assumed many different forms, they still retain similar roots and core elements. Although traditions are often invented or artificially revived, many customs and habits, even when suppressed, have persisted over long periods of time.

A few art forms are universal. Despite fundamental changes in aesthetic taste, we can still understand and appreciate literature and art and music from other periods and cultures. Although our primitive ancestors had fewer skills, different perceptions and far less knowledge, we probably still share with them similar instincts and emotions - fear, ambition, greed, anxiety, loyalty and grief. Some ideas, general principles and practices do not date, and remain valid so long as the problems which they address remain the same.

Each generation, however, faces a changed world and can only sustain the illusion of permanence by artifice. The assumptions and the rules that define a culture do not automatically renew; they need to be constantly reformulated and confirmed. The dominant features of the present – whether physical objects, like buildings, landscape and artifacts, or intellectual knowledge embedded in books or individual memory - only survive if they are saved, maintained and protected in libraries, museums, parks and educational institutions.

Once the shape of events has been firmly established, their origins and consequences need to be analyzed if we are to explain the evolution of the modern world. Otherwise the more that we know, the less we understand. Facts, although they often need correction and refinement, never change, but explanations drawn from the facts differ over time and are always subject to revision. The past is revealed by assembling facts, but understood through reflection, debate and imagination.

Major events have multiple simultaneous causes and different levels of causation. At one level, superficial or commonsense practical explanations may prove sufficient. At a deeper level, ideological, social, economic, and cultural forces - when codified as an integrated

theory - can provide a structural model of change.

The interaction of multiple events at different levels is harder to describe than individual facts. Causes have to be distinguished from symptoms and conditions. Factors, which operate in ways that are not easily verifiable, have to be inferred from their effects. Compiling population statistics, for example, is a numerical task, but explaining changes in the demographic structure requires an integrated theory. Malthusian checks will keep population and food supply in balance until demographic pressure forces improvements in technology and production.

Historians are able, if they so choose, to demonstrate what humans have achieved over the centuries. We can determine whether any situation, decision or policy in the past brought results that satisfied intentions. If we know the normal pattern of a repetitive cycle, we can identify a breakthrough when it occurs.

Nonetheless, History is only what we choose to recall from the past and that depends on present moods and inclinations. Each generation makes its own history and changes the past accordingly. If Society is just what people do, History is just what historians write. It is a story with many outcomes that were neither intended nor expected and it has to be retold in each generation. The truth can be discovered and learned, but it may not be what we expect to find or what we want to believe.

II   WHERE AND WHEN DID IT OCCUR?

Time never stands still, but whatever happens in history occurs at a particular place and at a particular moment. New centres of action emerge to replace those that recede into the past. Fixing events exactly in space and time gives them dimension and provides context. It allows them to be identified, measured and assessed. Comparing their relative significance then provides historical perspective.

History has always been determined by geography. **A limited** range of specific conditions determines where and when and in what form human life is viable. What people do, how often and on what scale depends on where they live. Their location might be mountain or desert, island or land mass, jungle or pasture, town square or countryside. The climate might be tropical or temperate, stormy or placid, dry or wet. The human presence can be either marginal or dense.

Different regions have different forms of agriculture, different social and political systems, different living habits and different rates of growth. Humans have tamed some physical environments,

but they are still dominated by others and constantly at the mercy of drought, disease, and natural disasters. We wrongly assume that people determine the history of particular areas or countries whereas it is often *vice versa*.

Events, ideas and habits all have spatial features. Certain places have long been permanent hubs of activity. Major historical developments usually occur at the centre rather than on the periphery. Wherever government is centralized, the metropolis develops a different lifestyle from the provinces. Some regions acquire strategic importance as military or naval points of entry or corridors - the Straits of Gibraltar, the Dardanelles, the Netherlands, the Alpine passes. Other regions enjoy economic advantages through geographical location or access to raw materials.

A major feature of global history is the contraction of space over time. Century by century, the world has narrowed and become closer, more crowded and more uniform. Religions and cultures have spread rapidly across the whole world. The same customs and events have emerged in many different places. The Earth has shrunk as the visible universe has grown. **The tyranny of distance and forced isolation has been gradually overcome and there is** closer and more frequent contact between cultures and lifestyles. Improved accessibility and the juxtaposition of populations has engendered similar solutions to shared problems, though **localism, tribalism and nationalism have also resisted globalization.**

An important motor of development in history has been the movement of people, whether through migration or conquest. Their distribution and redistribution has been both voluntary and compulsory and they have brought with them material resources, new technology and cosmopolitan ideas. Through intermarriage, integration, colonization and settlement humans have gradually altered the geography of the world, privileging certain languages, expanding opportunities and making heterogeneous cultures more homogeneous. At the same time, humans have become more dependent and remain prisoners of their environment.

Historians usually write about one place and they need to focus their efforts. Inevitably there is bias in their preferences. Because they like to study important events and issues, they gravitate to places where significant events are most likely to happen. Their choice is often the region or country that they inhabit. A high proportion of historical works are studies of the author's country or nation state. Some places are favored because they have expanding economies or enlightened cultures or have an unusual social and political structure.

Historians also need to choose a period to study. History has traditionally been divided into unwieldy chunks of time, initially determined by momentous events such as the fall of Rome, the fall of Constantinople or the French or Industrial Revolutions. Nowadays periodization is looser and more subtle and the criteria employed are more diffuse. The immediate past has more resonance than the distant past. **The time period usually reflects the range and type of questions that historians wish to**

pose and the source material at their disposal.

Some world histories roam through millenia and there is no limit in theory as to how far back in time historians can or need to reach to find explanations. The majority of historians, however, confine themselves to one or two centuries or less. They think in terms of human life expectancy and measure by generation. The duration of time - the distance between two points - is a relative measure. We treat institutions, religions and laws as immobile, because we compare their slow development with our relatively brief lives. **We regard the Earth as unchanging, because geological time is measured in millions of years.** But we are just applying a different time scale.

Time can move in cycles or follow a linear trajectory. Most historians adopt a linear approach, but people, societies, Empires and civilizations all have their own life cycle. They decay and renew, decline and fall. The old does evoke contradictory reactions. On the one

hand, age is venerated and equated with experience and wisdom. On the other hand, old fashioned facets of the past are dismissed as obsolescent. Curiosity and nostalgia do however promote awareness of the passage of time and a sense of history. The differences between past and present stimulate a search for origins.

The timing of events and the frequency with which they recur are often crucial. To understand an event, like a battle, historians must be able to visualize many actions simultaneously in different places. The number of times an event occurs is evidence of a trend and an indication of permanence. So much can depend on the timing of a meeting or the conjuncture of events. By identifying differences over time we can separate and classify stages of development.

Because historians have the advantage of hindsight, they can grasp the meaning of events better than contemporary witnesses, who are often unable to see the forest for the trees. Time creates perspective.

Those living through events cannot always see the reasons behind or the consequences of them. On the other hand, knowledge of what happens in the future can make it harder to understand the motives and expectations of those who lack that knowledge.

By examining how long it takes to develop we can measure the momentum of change. We can determine the time lag between the invention of an idea or technology and its acceptance and diffusion. The pace or rate of speed of change has accelerated over time; in each successive century everything happens faster and sooner. What took three generations to complete before the twentieth century now occurs in a decade.

Life is a continuum and change is incessant, irrevocable and perpetual. Nothing lasts forever. Routine and habit perpetuate old methods and ideas, but this does not prevent change. Time undermines our moral codes and alters our perception and attitudes. Styles, customs, standards and tastes are all ephemeral. Cultures are continually destroyed or transformed, along with their goals and value systems, by human conflicts and by economic and technological change. Sin, like treason, is a matter of dates.

We cannot reverse time and our former world has vanished forever. Nothing that happens in history repeats itself identically and we cannot replicate the past. Indeed human decisions have tended to swing like a pendulum from one extreme to the opposite. As adults or in old age we are not the same person that we were as children. No one has a life similar to anyone who lived in a previous period.

Because the passage of time erodes and alters values, what is significant in history changes constantly and is determined by frequency, duration, rarity and context. Time selects and justifies what is worthwhile and important. What matters in history is often a question of scale. Some features of the past, like the world in which we live, can sometimes be only seen with a microscope; at other times, a telescope is required. Fame only lasts as long as its audience and is often outlived by infamy. Even great achievements are fleeting, forgotten or down played. Only knowledge lasts and that has to be continuously refined.

  We all have to come to grips with the problem of time, to accept that what we have experienced as the present is now the past, that what we considered of vital importance is now forgotten or misunderstood, that what we

thought immutable and irreplaceable has succumbed to new ideas and methods.

III WHO BROUGHT IT ABOUT?

Have individuals or groups played a major role in the past or have historical events been principally determined by impersonal forces? Did people just react blindly to situations or did they act on their own initiative? Were their decisions rationally conceived or did they just surrender to their emotions? Do we control our own destiny and are we responsible for our actions?

Historians like to identify who was important and for what reasons, who to applaud and who to condemn. They compare the relative success or failure of individuals to see who came out on top? **Personal examples may be fascinating and worth examination, but they cannot speak for a whole population or society. They illustrate the particular, but they do not necessarily accurately represent the general.**

The great majority of living beings have left no trace, and the intentions and thoughts of those whose actions are known often remain a mystery. **Nor is it easy to appreciate attitudes and behaviour in cultures that are very different from our own. People so often do not know what to choose or what they want. Because human nature reacts strongly against any policy or belief that does not meet expectations, decisions have tended to veer between extremes.**

It is difficult for historians to identify and isolate the emotions behind actions; they are usually hidden from view and have to be inferred or deduced from expressed behaviour. Humans may claim and pretend to be rational, when they are actually emotionally driven, and their feelings often create conflicts of loyalty. But unearthing and calibrating emotions is crucial to understanding events and unexpected behaviour. Even when repressed, they are powerful forces which explain why people act in a particular way or fall victim to group hysteria.. Few decisions are made without some emotional input and expert manipulation of feelings can indoctrinate and prejudice whole populations . An otherwise inexplicable course of action or unwillingness to act can often be explained by anxiety or hatred , by disgust or nostalgia, by anger or possessiveness. Fear can create or exaggerate threats and take many forms - fear of damnation, fear of other groups in society, fear of new ideas or customs. The joker in the pack can just be a change of mood.

History seems so often to certify the follies of humankind. Knowledge of past errors rarely prevents anyone from repeating the same mistakes. Expectations often outrun resources and knowledge. Nothing seems permanently to discredit unattainable ends or to discourage recourse to violence. Contact with other cultures does not necessarily lead to greater tolerance and understanding. The rigidity of both religious and secular belief systems has proved a

serious obstacle to the advance of knowledge.

Mass education has consistently failed to advance self knowledge or to eliminate ignorance, hypocrisy or prejudice. Whole nations have succumbed with blind faith to the appeal of charisma and emotion. Throughout history people have been willing to pursue inconsistent ends and to ignore any contradictions between their principles and practice.

Intellectuals tend to dislike and minimize the importance of individual agency, because humans are too complex, too diverse, too volatile, too subjective and too difficult to predict to reconcile with or accommodate to grand theory. They fear the irrational and the non rational, abhor whim, impulse and animal spirits, and prefer to argue deductively from first principles. Theologians identify the passions with original sin and believe that individuals should observe moral precepts, not indulge their personal choices. Economists prefer to design mathematical models in which people maximize their utility. Administrators want people to obey directions rather than follow their own code of conduct and pursue their private interests.

Emotions release many anti-social attitudes and can provoke sudden changes and disorder. What people like is not necessarily what is good for them or in the public interest. Easily distracted and diverted from the central issues, they often display poor judgment and act foolishly. So enlightened thinkers stress

Interest rather than passion, calculation rather than feeling, control rather than instinct. They recommend a consistent, hard headed, precise, clear, rational approach which argues from evidence. Whatever, the ultimate objective, a cool head is preferred to a warm heart.

The real alternative, however, is not so much reason versus emotion, as one emotion versus another. Each is defined by its opposite - disgust versus empathy, aggression versus submissiveness, grief versus joy, anger versus despair, enthusiasm versus disappointment, envy versus sympathy, suspiciousness versus trust. The true danger lies in extremes of feeling, not in the feelings themselves. So bold becomes reckless, and caution becomes inertia, love becomes infatuation, fear becomes paranoia. Sometimes people move from one extreme to the other. Pure feelings are probably less important than personality characteristics such as greed, scepticism, stoicism, shyness,

honesty, indiscretions or resoluteness.

The early historians were captivated by heroic individuals and deeds, and celebrity worship is still a feature of historical biography. Even if we reject the cult of the great man in history, **it is clear that exceptional men and women have made a huge difference. Hundreds of military and political leaders, organizers, writers, artists, scientists, and thinkers, have displayed unusual and innovative talents.**

We can respect and prioritize their impressive operations and careers and admire their willingness to fight to the death or risk their lives in the pursuit of fame or knowledge or improved conditions for humanity. **It is important that proactive entrepreneurs should emerge who are willing to create opportunities instead of waiting for them to appear. Only individuals who are mobile and willing to act spontaneously will overcome inertia** and venture beyond traditional boundaries.

The lone genius may pave the way, but we must not forget that hundreds of thousands of individuals, who were neither members of the elite nor of the male gender, have also made vital contributions. Ordinary people, who followed their leaders, eschewed change and just discharged their duties, have still been instrumental in protecting the *status quo*. The routine services that they mechanically perform have been essential to support and maintain the whole system.

Even if most people leave nothing behind them of great importance, they still maintain the life cycle and breed and train the next generation. They are content to pass on their genes and experience to future generations. **Individual effort is crucial, but collective struggle and combined actions are also responsible for great achievements. Cooperation has proved important and it is the interaction between people and**

their cumulative efforts that have usually proved successful.

IV WHAT WAS THE DRIVING FORCE?

Do humans enjoy any control over their future? To believers in scientific history, everything is determined not by individuals, but by impersonal forces. Marx and his followers and imitators envisaged a world governed by iron economic and social laws, similar to those of natural science. Neo-conservatives believe that the market fixes everything without intervention.

It is certainly true that non-human forces explain much of world history. Population levels, for example, are determined by infertility, disease, and food supply. Migration is hardly a choice, when the alternative is death or extreme poverty. The impact of climate change, epidemics or economic depression dwarfs that of human actions.

Humans also initiate events and then lose control of them. They start wars and revolutions, which acquire a life of their own and prove to be longer, more deadly and more chaotic than expected. Even when they attain their principal objectives, they have to face unexpected consequences. Solving one problem, particularly in technology, usually just creates another. Circumstances combine to create a new force that has its own momentum.

Individual agency, exercising free will, is necessarily unpredictable, because any human decision is influenced by personality, upbringing and environment. No one has a choice about where or when they are born. Our genes determine who we are and what we are capable of achieving during our lives. Our free will is limited and our plans have unintended outcomes.

    Nevertheless, our actions still help to determine the future. Despite being subject to forces outside our control we are still able to sway our destiny, to respond to changing circumstances by refining our inherited skills and adapting them to meet new needs. We are even able to explore and understand how our universe functions.

Many natural forces can be manipulated, if not controlled by human intervention. The level of population can be modulated by human action, by the age of marriage, by war, and by contraception. Although governed by Nature, we interact with our environment, both changing it and being changed by it.

In what ways are people responsible for

their actions? They are certainly offspring of a particular culture, but some can rise above it and select what they believe and how they should act. They can invent and follow a moral code and choose to be responsible for what they do. The weight of tradition fosters inertia, but some can emancipate themselves and challenge or change the value system. Even in the distant past, when tyranny, slavery and genocide were widely tolerated, there were those who condemned these practices and advocated the sanctity of human life and the right to liberty.

Historians want, and their readers expect, the past to be explained in definite and objective terms and this leads towards abstraction and determinism. They embrace models and theories which, as in the natural sciences, try to advance knowledge and understanding in an orderly and dispassionate way. Deductive reasoning becomes the preferred way of explaining whatever occurs, including all human actions. Events are determined by factors other than human feelings, because emotions are too complex and unpredictable.

The origin and development of emotions can, of course, be rationally identified and explained; they are biologically determined and culturally constructed. The primal emotions derive from a congenital instinct for self preservation; feelings are defined and channeled and encouraged or suppressed by social and religious institutions. Cultures maintain social harmony and personal stability by controlling human passions. Some emotions are not universal or shared by everyone. INor do individuals necessarily exhibit the same feelings in the same way. Their range and intensity and precise operation vary between different cultures.

Time and place are also variables. The same emotions are not equally characteristic of all societies, regions and periods . Their meaning and significance vary with age, upbringing, and social needs and priorities. Some emotions acquire a different value or occur with greater frequency or intensity in particular periods or particular groups in society. The emotional reactions of people are provoked and heightened by particular circumstances and by uncertainty.

If it is true that human decisions affect, even if they do not on their own determine, historical events then it matters how and when and what they feel. If the senses allow humans to function, their emotions determine their behavior, maintain order and sustain them in the face of adversity. Whether initiating or reacting to events, human decisions are always personal. They may be reached by rational choice and by dispassionate analysis, but hatred and contempt start and sustain conflicts and preempt and warp policies. Altruism and comradeship, on the other hand, keep families and communities together and provide assistance and reassurance. Humans are moved and inspired by suffering and grief and spurred to action by bravery and boldness, by love and loyalty, by generosity and comradeship.   Their emotions create the incentive and provide the strength to persist, innovate and recover from disasters..

It is also the emotions that generate and maintain ideas, principles, policies, ideologies and works of art. Sometimes the effect is negative, as when fear or

patriotism or anarchism lead to restlessness, violence, discrimination and intolerance. But without hope, longing, enthusiasm, and dreams, reason alone cannot create a new world. Historians are themselves subject to the same emotions that have always influenced people. They feel as well as think; they can pursue or ignore the glories and the horrors of the past. Like those they study, they can be obsessed with order, seduced by beauty, or driven by an insatiable desire to improve . What they narrate and interpet can reflect guilt or empathy, fervor or cynicism, scorn or devotion,

zeal for the truth or blind adherence to the status quo.

The Earth had a history, governed by its own laws, long before the human species even appeared. But its history over the past few centuries is incomprehensible without acknowledging individual agency and that means recognizing the relevance and importance of what humans feel. People have changed the world as well as being changed by it. They make their own history, even if it does not always materialize as they wish.

V WHETHER IT SHOULD BE PRESERVED OR CONDEMNED?

Some features of the past have survived continuous change because we honor and preserve so many customs and artifacts. Who decides what to keep and what criteria do they employ? Is what survives real or artificial? Should we judge the past by the standards of the present? Can we hold those, who lived in a different period and culture with different values, responsible for their actions?

Whole cultures and lifestyles disappear as the economy and the world change. But because everyone adapts rapidly to their environment, people can easily miss the significance of changes in their own lifetime. One of the great advantages of studying the past is that it reveals the direction and the magnitude of change. By looking back and by comparison, we can measure what has changed and judge whether it has been for better or worse. What History provides is perspective.

Each generation, however, has to decide how much of the past should be remembered and which features are worth preserving. Civilizations on the decline usually look backwards, whereas those on the rise look forwards. The old has less cachet in self confident, expanding societies. Achievements lose their relevance when fame is undermined by changes in what is considered significant.

    The fascination that the past still exercises can be explained by curiosity, pride or nostalgia for

what has formerly been achieved. The monuments that are built or retained both define and honor past success. Sometimes what is omitted from stories of the past is more significant than what is promulgated.

Historians are expected to select and justify what is important, to choose which ideas, customs, memories or art forms are worth perpetuating forever? As might be expected, they have differed drastically over time as to which aspects should be selected or emphasized. When writing history, exceptional events, such as battles or revolutions or watersheds, always take center place. The great discoveries of travelers and scientists are also lauded as are the creative peaks of literature and art. But many fundamental developments and innovations are overlooked.

Living too much in former times can be counter productive. The past is different from and often compares unfavorably with the present. Much of what we consider

important may have meant nothing in earlier periods and will be disregarded or dismissed in the future. Since history is primarily written by the victors, it is their interests and values which tend to be justified and commemorated.

The criteria that define importance change over time. The customs, standards, rules and styles that are promulgated and prized in one period are condemned or dismissed as trivial or immoral in another. Traditions are often artificial and have to be transmitted or reinvented. Although the most important contributions of the arts and sciences have usually survived, sometimes through revivals, what is considered to have social or aesthetic or moral value changes frequently. Shakespeare or Rembrandt have not always been held in high esteem. Importance is always related to subject and need.

Fashion just happens and often determines what is in and out, what is remembered and revered and what is forgotten, and it is as ruthless as it is unpredictable.

People tend to adopt, rather than choose, a fashion. A trend can emerge and be followed without having any clear direction or purpose. As in the garment industry, someone designs something new, others imitate it and then it just loses support and is discarded. When a fashionable artifact or custom is revised or revived, the style is never absolutely the same.

We have to recognize that people in the past lived and acted by moral standards which they

considered correct, even if they are unacceptable to us now. All ethical standards are relative and subjective; neither beauty nor virtue is absolute or universal. There is only limited consensus as to which values are appropriate in which context under which circumstances.

We can still, however, examine critically the arguments which contemporaries advanced both to justify and to reject practices, such as slavery, which we now find abhorrent. When we discuss the attitudes and behavior of colonists in the heyday of European Imperialism, we can distinguish between condescension towards the indigenous inhabitants (which might still have beneficial effects) and outright exploitation.

Some values have staying power and offer some solution to moral dilemmas. History bears witness to the slow, but impressive, growth of humanitarian values. Many basic rights and obligations – to food, shelter and care - were asserted far back in the past, though the emphasis has increased in more recent times.

We can also recognize, without condoning it, that circumstances are sometimes to blame for brutality and cruelty. Difficulties with enforcement can explain extreme penalties, like capital punishment for trivial crimes. Conditions sometimes justify authoritarian government. Even though the laws may be harsh and the state repressive, the rule of law may still be preferable to the tyranny of local warlords or to anarchy.

    Historians are probably right to cast blame in cases where contemporaries wittingly did harm, when they knew what was wrong and could have behaved better. Although it is probably unfair to condemn as immoral someone indoctrinated from birth, we can praise those who examined and then tried to eliminate the worst rules and prejudices of their day. We can applaud those who, given an alternative, chose the better one.

History is neutral or amoral, but historians still need to distinguish good from evil. Every event or innovation or decision has both a moral upside and downside, often unintended. Judgment is of course subjective and will vary with age and experience. But we cannot avoid taking sides, if only indirectly or vicariously, when we compare the spiritual and material differences between the past and the present. Often the issues and problems that arise are moral rather than technical. Democracy,

for example, may be less efficient in some contexts, than oligarchy or tyranny but it can still be regarded as morally superior.

It is possible to denounce evil and condemn error while still recognizing that in earlier periods people inherited and followed different standards. Some will adopt as their standard the utility of the greatest number; others might argue for quality of life or spirit. Despite a common tendency to applaud celebrities, such as soldier Emperors, we can condemn

the pursuit of power through conquest unless it leads to better government.

Everyone should expect to be criticized in the present or in the future for making poor judgments. We need, on the one hand, to reflect on the mistakes that have been made and what they have cost and, on the other hand, to appreciate wiser decisions that have yielded benefits. What the past so often demonstrates is that humankind has been more successful at increasing its knowledge than at acquiring wisdom or righting wrongs.

One of the more alarming consequences of studying history is to discover that evil men can and have prospered without suffering any remorse or punishment. It is the most adaptable and skilful who survive, not the most moral. Not only is justice frequently delayed or dismissed in this world, but there is probably no Hell to punish the wicked. The only consolation is that evil deeds can sometimes have beneficial results. War, greed, acquisitiveness and exploitation, for example, can concentrate capital, accelerate inventions, and spur economic growth.

What should we retain from the past? We can accept that change is inevitable, but still desire to keep the best features of the past and expect them to continue. We want to preserve our own life's work and hope that we have contributed something of lasting benefit and will be remembered for it.

What criteria, however, should we apply when we judge the past? We can admire vision, stamina, skill and imagination, while deploring inhumanity. We should try to comprehend people and events, not to condemn them, to explain, but not to excuse them. Understanding our forebears is not easy, but it makes no greater demands on our imagination and sensibility than having to adjust to the frequent and fundamental refashioning of society and culture in our own day.

VI HOW DID IT DEVELOP?

Before we ask why, we have to ask how. History, the story of humankind, unfolds as a sequence of events; one fact or occurrence leads to another. This process can be viewed either backwards or forwards. It can be understood by just describing, step by step, what actually happened. The quality of the evidence determines the accuracy of the description, not the reasoning or judgment of the author.

Historians first have to identify the facts that explain how an event was able to occur before they can try to identify its cause. As in a crime scene, any event has to be reconstructed and a timeline established before investigators or prosecutors can discover and prove a motive. So a satisfactory account of the D Day landings in Normandy would describe exactly how the troops landed on shore and fought their way inland before asking whether or not there might be a better method of invasion or why the assault was successful.

Most historical narratives need to devote much of their space to describing the basic mechanics of life in the chosen period, because both the way that the economy functions and the goods and services that are available differ from the present day. Older systems of agriculture, manufacturing, transport, and finance are often unrecognizable. Houses, ships, equipment and food are just not designed, produced, delivered, maintained or consumed in the same way. The further back in time we travel, the greater the differences or the omissions. Indeed conditions are often so harsh and the obstacles so great that it is difficult to understand how anyone could have survived.

How people lived is chiefly a factual question. For most periods, it is possible to establish without any doubt how they ate, dressed, talked and played, how they treated sickness and death, how they handled marriage and parenting, how they relaxed and socialized, how each generation was educated and trained and acquired self knowledge. Historians can usually reconstruct with ease the manners and customs of a society and how it was structured, how each social or occupational class had its own role and expectations and how it accepted or rejected the others.

A simple factual account of the political narrative is more difficult, because it is volatile and often controversial and therefore requires judgment. But it is possible to describe without challenge how a country or state is governed - its constitution, laws and customs, its central and local administration, the corridors and channels and levers of power. It is not difficult to describe the bureaucratic process of an administration - how the peace is kept, how orders are given and executed, how laws are made and enforced, how policy is actually decided.

Similarly, the instruments and the methods of organizing and conducting warfare on sea and land can easily be recounted.

It is usually enough just to relate how a situation evolved. All we need in order to admire and comprehend the great conquests of human history is a narrative account. So we listen to the story of how Alexander the Great created in ten years an Empire that stretched from Greece to India. We learn how the Anglo-Saxon King Harold managed to fight one battle at Stamford Bridge and then immediately march south 300 miles to fight another at Hastings. We discover how Henan Cortes conquered the Aztec Empire or Francisco Pizarro subdued the Inca Empire with a handful of men.

The same is true of exploration and settlement. The astonishing distances that travelers and migrants have been able to cover in the past speak for themselves. It is not surprising that migrants from Europe would eventually colonize North and South America, or that improved technology would allow tropical Africa, the Himalayas or Antarctica to be explored. But it is fascinating to learn how Marco Polo made his way to China or the Vikings to Sicily and North America or the nomads of central Asia to both China and Europe. We can appreciate the range of human qualities that made these remarkable feats possible - resourcefulness, pugnacity, valor, endurance, persistence, and loyalty.

We can also see, looking back, how scientific knowledge has been applied to improve technology and vice versa; need stimulates and promotes innovative methods and those methods in turn contribute to understanding the science. It is easy to demonstrate how technology expands basic human faculties and skills.

Energy is harnessed and increased to replace human labor, to revolutionize everything from domestic tools to transport to weapons of war. The diseases of humans are identified and cured, their bones mended, their lives extended and their bodies improved and maintained. Improvements in livestock and arable farming increase the quantity and quality of food, which is also better cooked and stored. Housing is made more comfortable with better heating, lighting and furniture. As methods of communication become faster and more reliable, knowledge spreads more widely and efficiently.

Technology has a built-in momentum; its effects become causes. Greater privacy, for example, is made possible by the subdivision of rooms. and that subdivision creates a demand for greater privacy. The process of technological change is continuous. Each innovation, once introduced, leads to another, either through refinement of technique or because a new problem is created, which has to be solved. In warfare, for example, new weapons of attack provoke new defenses which in turn provoke new weapons.

Breakthroughs in technology often occur when all ways of improving the old methods have been exhausted. To understand how the world develops, it is necessary to explore the dialectical relationship between innovation and continuity. When change is planned and initiated by the entrepreneur, it usually provokes resistance, because most societies will fight to protect the *status quo*. Routine maintenance is also necessary to keep any social system or political Empire functioning. But over time novel methods and ideas are gradually accepted and become a new norm; what has been changed now has to be defended and preserved. Without experimentation, there can be no improvement, but any change needs to be stabilized and balanced to survive.

Much of what happens in history is just a natural process. The course of events has consequences that are not caused by human action or choice. Most knowledge advances in linear fashion, building on past successes. Each stage is the natural result of past development and in its turn generates the next stage forwards. Description of how anything happens can thus become an explanation. It is an exaggeration to claim that the British Empire was acquired in a fit of absence of mind, but territory was just slowly accumulated, by accident as well as by design. The domination of the world by European countries or the colonization of the American West has been alleged by devotees to be a natural or divinely ordained destiny.

The same events repeat so often that **historians are able to generalize about patterns of behavior or how impersonal forces** operate. Although history, unlike natural science, has no laws, in particular situations certain features can be expected to recur without human intervention. Any military, economic or intellectual lead or advantage, for example, is only temporary. Revolutions free up talent and provide opportunities that do not exist under normal conditions. Wars increase in scale and ferocity over time and gradually involve the whole population. All radical reforms eventually rigidify, but all bureaucracies need an informal core, if they are to retain flexibility. Every society exploits its poor and servile and their revolts rarely succeed. An elite may be replaced, but the new elite still monopolizes wealth and power.

By observing how the world has developed historians can judge whether or not this represents progress. Usually progress is equated with a higher standard of living and measured quantitatively – a longer, more comfortable and more secure life, more material

goods, faster transportation, smarter technology and more effective medicine.

More efficient farming methods have certainly increased the food supply and reduced human suffering. **The optimist can also cite the breathtaking** progress in all branches of knowledge, thought and expression over the centuries. Looking back, we can see how dazzling intellects have revolutionized astronomy, science and medicine, how imagination, originality and vision have transformed literature, the arts and music across the world.

We can admire these enormous accomplishments, but the real test of progress is qualitative. Has the world that humans created become a more humane and enlightened place? Do **a greater percentage of people live fuller and more virtuous lives? Have war, tyranny, poverty, disease, injustice, inequality or prejudice disappeared? Have we lost civility and tranquility?**

Unfortunately greater knowledge and smarter technology have not changed human nature, including its dark side. Methods of killing, for example, have dramatically improved but without any reduction in bellicosity and aggression. Progress is always offset by an equivalent or worse downside – two steps forwards, one step back. All human advances have negative features; a better mousetrap is not better for the mouse. We face enormous environmental issues and our very

solutions breed new problems - disease, pollution, and overpopulation, to name just a few. More efficient farming may feed more people now, but it can destroy the habitat in the long term.

On balance, however, progress is not a myth, if we define it in terms of what has definitely been achieved or improved. **Whether these advances will continue into the next generation or extend to everyone is of course another matter.** Despite its great faults, humanity has learned over time how to use its resources more efficiently. Our awareness of progress, however, depends on looking back to see how the world has evolved. It is History that allows us to judge what has worked and what has not. Without being able to access the past we would, like medieval people, have no concept of progress.

Historians in their efforts to give coherence to the past will always tend to highlight the decisive factors. Sometimes it will be a particular fact; at other times, the

crucial explanation may be a long term factor such as naval power or geographical location or technological supremacy. Whatever the scale of the problem, it is much easier and probably wiser and more productive just to reconstruct how events occurred and not attempt to explain why they happened. We can explain how, without having to explain why.

VI I WHY DID IT HAPPEN?

Historians can demonstrate how events unfolded, but they cannot offer irrefutable reasons as to why they took place or why some did not happen or persist. A finite number of explanations rotate over the years, often in circles, with the emphasis shifting from one to another, but none ever proves conclusive. Any explanation is always contested, because it necessarily involves judgments

about value, significance, and emphasis.

In some cases historians are able to identify causes which are necessary, but not sufficient. In other cases, such as the economic interpretation of social change, they can connect cause and effect, but not demonstrate the precise mechanism that links them. In other cases, they can identify who generated a creative theory or policy or work of art, but cannot explain why someone should have had the idea or found the inspiration.

The search for explanation in history is always retrospective. We look backwards to reconstruct events and their origins without considering what would be an infinite number of alternatives. It is more feasible to explain the past, when we know what happened, because we do not have to explain why anything failed to occur.

Since any event will have multiple causes, the alternatives must be weighed to measure their relative importance. Ever since Aristotle postulated four main types of cause, a fundamental distinction has been made between material or efficient causes, which explain the process and sequence of events, and formal or final causes which explain their direction and purpose. To understand why anything happens, it can be argued, we have to know its purpose as well as its mechanism.

The human species diverged fundamentally and irreversibly from other forms of life when some of its members began to search for meaning in the universe. Although they had been programmed to preserve themselves and perpetuate their species, they were not content just to survive. As their cognitive skills developed, they acquired new goals and wanted to know who they were and why they existed. This questioning arose partly from curiosity and partly because a knowable and certain destiny was reassuring to a vulnerable species whose progeny had to be nurtured for a long period.

But what could that end be? Many elaborate theories of history have been constructed to answer this question. Those who believe in an omnipotent Deity argue that everything that has happened is intentional and has a Divine purpose. Other candidates for the role of final end have included the city state, the nation state, tribes and ethnic groups, the classless society, liberal democracy, and free market capitalism. All these teleologies had some kind of ethic embedded and they assumed or implied inevitable progress towards a higher goal. The final end was a moral end and had its roots in or was logically derived from some compulsion or vision in the present. What ought to be was more important than what was.

To a certain extent, this quest for meaning is justified because it provides humanity with a reason to strive. **If history is just one damn fact after another, a process of evolution towards an unknown end, then people have no incentive to learn or to improve. By inventing or borrowing myths, they can give their lives a purpose and a goal to achieve.**

Some answers could be inferred from the world around them, but to find the *raison d'être* of humankind, it was necessary to explore and analyze the past as well as the present. If History had no purpose, then human lives were meaningless. History to the philosopher, Hegel, was the logical development of an Idea. Some theories, such as Marxism, even had stages of development, which usually conflicted. The ultimate result was achieved by the clash of opposing forces.

Many early theories, influenced probably by the visible reappearance of the sun, the cycle of life and death and the natural order of the seasons, adopted a static and cyclical model which had no final end. The end became the beginning with the completion of the cycle. The linear development of technology, social structures and institutions, however, made thinkers aware of change, that humans had a history and linear history implies direction and purpose. Those who wished to believe that men and women had evolved for a reason were persuaded to credit change over time with a final purpose. Surely, they argued, the cumulative actions and events of the past must constitute and reveal a particular goal.

The long dominance of this teleological approach is easy to explain. Historians of a religious bent, who were eager to find eternal truths and affirm immortal life, could envisage the history of the world as the unfolding of the Divine Will. More secular historians could embrace philosophies, such as the Whig interpretation, in which England from its earliest days moved irrevocably over time towards middle class values and representative government. The ends attributed to History, have usually proved to be vague, boring and time-bound, rather like traditional concepts of Heaven or of any Utopia.

In their search for meaning, philosophers have mistakenly reified History. The narrative of past events has been erroneously given a concrete structure which is capable of action and even contemplation. Despite the convenience of employing History as a shorthand label, it is a deceptive term. History is both a factual record of past events in chronological order and at the same time a selection from and analysis of those events. But it cannot promote or pursue any goal. It is an abstraction without any physical properties or purpose.

The development of humankind has completely outdistanced all other species. But in many respects the history of humans is not fundamentally different from the evolution of plants and animals and fish. Evolution is essentially the product of trial and error plus time. New forms develop automatically and

continuously, as the environment changes and forces continuous adaptation.

Humans have always been both pushed by the need to survive and pulled by any opportunity to better the conditions of their existence. Since evolution is continuous and irreversible, it must develop in a particular direction and its primary end is greater efficiency. Changes also have consequences and acquire a purpose by just happening. Technology also moves only in one

direction - towards greater efficiency - and it never travels backwards. The bow does not replace the gun.

If humans have a purpose, it is to maintain and improve their skills and security by exploring and manipulating their environment. They possess a relentless drive towards efficiency, greater complexity and greater self consciousness, and they validate their efforts by the outcome. What begins as a struggle for existence turns into material improvement.

Natural curiosity and resourcefulness lead to greater knowledge and smarter technology.

One goal which humanity has always had, and which is programmed at birth, is the preservation and perpetuation of the species. As individuals and in groups, humans have always struggled to reproduce and improve their skills, resources and environment through adaptation. As a priority, they nourish and train their children to become the next generation. This task has been extended to protect the group to which they belong - destroying rivals, securing territory and developing a culture.

It is tempting to imagine and to hope that human lives have a purpose apart from self preservation, to believe that understanding all aspects of our universe is an end in itself. The pursuit of knowledge is important, but it is the search for meaning that really drives us hardest. History has its own logic. We explain the present by working back through the past only to find that meaning is subjective and relative. What we determine to be necessary is rarely sufficient. Why is a crooked letter and no explanation is ever final.

EPILOGUE

IS HISTORY CREATED BY ACCIDENT OR BY DESIGN?

Although Einstein was unwilling to accept that anything happens by chance, the cosmologists tell us that the universe is programmed for disorder, that even the basic elements and forces are not universal. Gravity, light and time can be distorted and, according to the law of entropy, there may not be sufficient energy to restore order. Ultimately, all the great achievements of humanity – the outstanding literature and art that it has produced, the huge advances in knowledge and technology, its whole history – will be lost.

In every place and time, the unexpected and the never expected and the unintended have continuously occurred. The course of history has been diverted or changed by arbitrary and often trivial factors. The mathematician and philosopher of the seventeenth century Blaise Pascal highlighted this truth in a famous pensée: "si le nez de Cléopâtre eût été plus court, toute la face du monde aurait changé". In the twentieth century, Heisenberg demonstrated the principle of uncertainty by proving that the position and the velocity of an object cannot both be measured exactly at the same time.

Events can also be determined by circumstances which occur randomly. The role of chance is self evident, but frequently underestimated. A cataclysm, like the meteor impact which wiped out the dinosaurs, might be a freakish event, unlikely to occur very often. But luck or bad luck is always present.

Opportunities are created by being in the right place at the right time. How many generals never have their opportunity to shine because they are killed in action too early in their careers? Sometimes a trivial factor, like a chance meeting or failure to meet, has disproportionate and decisive consequences.

The role of chance in human history is irrefutable. Where and when humans live determines who they are and what they do and how they develop. Their health and longevity is always subject to random natural forces. Chance determines which individuals are present at any time, their temperament, beliefs and skills and therefore which choices they make. Fashion follows no law. When events are determined by economic or cultural forces, by chance or by physical laws like gravity, they have no moral content, unlike decisions and choices made by free will.

Sometimes circumstances can combine fortuitously. Luck and opportunity are certainly as necessary as skill when fighting a battle or seizing power. How many artists and men and women of genius never had the chance to perform? The timing of a crucial *conjuncture* of events is frequently accidental. The presence or absence of a particular person or factor at a decisive moment is often pure chance. Minor events can have major consequences.

This does not mean that the course of events cannot be predicted at all or that they do not follow recognizable patterns. If time is infinite, anything and everything will happen eventually. Patterns do recur and can be predicted with high probability. Indeed medical science depends heavily on statistics. We know that an acorn in the ground can only become an oak tree, even though we do not know whether it will grow or how large it will become or how long it will live. In retrospect, the history or herstory of humankind is fundamentally an evolutionary process. Humans have been mere spectators of events for millions of years and, even in historic times, they have been forced to be reactive as well as proactive. But whoever and whatever has proved most successful at adapting to changing circumstances has come out ahead.

Historians and philosophers have always been reluctant to admit chance and have offered alternative explanations. The Ancients mythologized chance as Fate and

were happy to ascribe events to some deity pulling the strings. Einstein was unable to accept cosmic disorder and never abandoned his belief that there was some, as yet, unformulated law or laws that would explain indeterminacy.

The overriding factor behind this reluctance seems to be fear of uncertainty. The desire to reduce the world to order and coherence is powerful and widespread. People struggle to predict because they need to know what to expect. It is not a known risk, but uncertainty that roils financial markets.

There have always been determinists who prefer to believe that history is predictable (if not fully pre-determined) and not the result of accident or human decision. Their theoretical models usually predicate systematic and irresistible forces like the economic and social determinism of Marxism. Events follow a generalized pattern, even if there are many variations, and they move consistently towards a specific (and usually enlightened) goal such as democracy, higher living standards, equality, peaceful co-existence or greater knowledge. It is not only in the natural sciences that general principles apply universally and over time. The political and military advice of the Ancients still works in a modern context.

Opportunities are created as well as seized by proactive planning, and, even when they appear by chance, someone has to take advantage of them and correct deficiencies and unintended consequences. The genius may appear and survive by accident, but major innovations and discoveries usually appear in clusters at the same time. So often in human history the breakthrough point of knowledge occurs just when it is most needed. Technology evolves constantly and cumulatively and has a built-in momentum which eventually reaches critical mass.

So it is true that everything happens by chance and equally true that everything evolves in orderly progression. Like the physical universe, human history is subject to chaos and uncertainty and yet governed by identifiable and measurable forces. We can accurately predict the length of days or the movements of the tides, but events are still determined by random factors and we can only estimate the probability of anything happening based on past experience.

    Actuaries cannot determine how or when any one individual will die, but, given a large group, they can accurately predict the lifespan of a high percentage. Most events in history have evolved from a prior situation and combined with random factors. Although some lives follow what seem to be predictable paths, no one can know for certain what their future will be.

The course of history is determined in the short term by chance and free will and in the long term by fundamental inert forces. Random factors can halt, redirect, slow or quicken the march of events, which follow an otherwise predictable course. Reconstructing process, however, only provides a partial explanation: *post hoc* does not necessarily mean *propter hoc.*

Humans thrive on chaos and uncertainty; the unexpected and unintended promote innovation. The paradox of chance versus determinism has positive consequences. Indeed without uncertainty there would be no progress. Order and stability are maintained in human society, as in the natural world, through mutual dependence and by balancing interests and needs. International relations seek a balance of power just as the market seeks equilibrium.

But too rigid a balance can generate a perpetual *status quo*. Evolution over time will cumulatively improve efficiency through experience and adaptation, but it is new knowledge that punctuates equilibrium and initiates change. Technology is the exogenous factor which, though it occasionally pauses or retreats, moves forward continuously and prevents stasis.

To try and understand the past is to confront paradox after paradox. We can only see it through the eyes of the present, no matter how hard we try to divest ourselves of bias. Random factors constantly upend the smooth course of history. The balance of forces that maintain stability needs continuous adjustment. The pursuit of greater efficiency and knowledge is both an end and a means. Standards of value are absolute and universal in theory and relative and particular in practice. Each advance contains the seeds of future problems. In short, the dominant feature of human history is contradiction.

We can explain how the world has changed, but not why or for what purpose, if any. The past, however, provides a standard to grade our behavior and objectives and progress. We rely on it to learn what has worked and we seek to refine and apply that knowledge to create a better future. Attempts to predict the future are invariably wrong, because the number of possible factors and combinations of factors is overwhelming. We can project from the past and calculate the probability of what might happen, but that is still speculative. **We cannot command the future, and if we could, life would be intolerable. Historians do not find certainties; they travel hopefully, but they never arrive at their destination.**

The Past talks incessantly,

the present chooses what to hear,

and the future never speaks at all.

HISTORICAL WORKS BY RICHARD GRASSBY

A New Dictionary of British History, ed. S. H. Steinberg and I. H. Evans (1st ed. 1963, 2nd ed. 1970)

"Social Mobility and Commercial Enterprise in Seventeenth Century England," in *Puritans and Revolutionaries*, ed. K. V. Thomas and D. Pennington (Oxford University Press, 1979), 355-81

"Social Status and Commercial Enterprise under Louis XIV," *Economic History Review*, 2nd ser.,

13 (1960), reprinted in *State and Society in Seventeenth Century France*, ed. R. F. Kierstead (New York, 1975)

The English Gentleman in Trade: The Life and Works of Sir Dudley North 1641-1691 (Oxford University Press, 400 pages, 1994)

Ship Sea and Sky: the Marine Art of James Edward Buttersworth 1817-1894 (Rizzoli International, 128 pages, 1994)

The Business Community of Seventeenth Century England

(Cambridge University Press, 618 pages, 1995)

The Idea of Capitalism before the Industrial Revolution (Roman and Littlefield, 125 pages, 1999)

Kinship and Capitalism: Marriage, Family and Business in the English-Speaking World, 1580-1740 (Woodrow Wilson Center Press and Cambridge University Press, 505 pages, 2001)

The Oxford Dictionary of National Biography, ed. H. C. G. Matthew and B. Harrison (Oxford, 2004) Contributing author

The Biographical Dictionary of British Economists, ed. D. Rutherford, 2 vols (Bristol, 2004) Contributing author

Rhetoric and Reality: Culture and Society in early modern Britain (Amazon, 445 pages, 2016, 2017)

Money to Burn: Lifestyles of the business community of early modern Britain, 2 vols 951 pages (Amazon, 2016)

A Scholar's Tale: Reminiscences of a peripatetic historian (Amazon, 98 pages, 2017)

Made in the USA
Columbia, SC
22 March 2023

29345a5b-f5f5-4126-a8e6-0e38b3b8fb2eR01